WELCOME TO MINEWORLD MINECRAFT ACTIVITIES

PACKED TO THE WITHER WITH AMAZING PUZZLES, GAMES AND FACTS!

WORDSEARCH!

1. Can you find the Minecraft-related words in our wordsearch? You'll need your hunting skills to find some of them!

H	X	Z	O	M	B	I	E	A	H
C	O	C	E	L	O	T	H	S	V
R	C	V	F	Z	Z	L	I	Y	Z
A	G	R	W	M	F	F	G	Z	B
F	B	U	E	U	R	S	X	X	Z
T	M	I	N	E	C	R	A	F	T
I	S	G	V	W	P	R	U	C	U
N	V	L	Y	O	D	E	E	I	N
G	I	R	Z	S	W	O	R	D	B
S	F	R	E	D	S	T	O	N	E

CRAFTING   OCELOT   SWORD

CREEPER   REDSTONE   ZOMBIE

MINECRAFT   SILVERFISH

SPOT THE DIFFERENCE

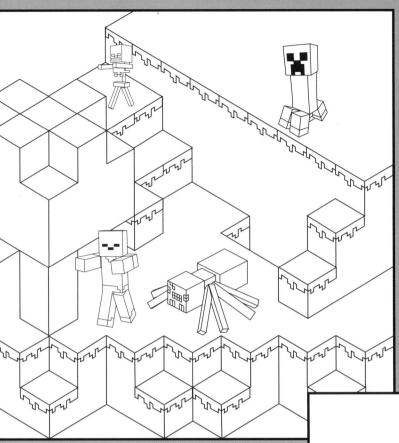

2. Can you spot five differences between the top and bottom images?

Did you Know!? 'Mobs' is short for 'mobile'? The mobs in these pictures are just a handful of the baddies you find sneaking around in Minecraft!

3.

Draw a line from dot to dot to complete the picture!

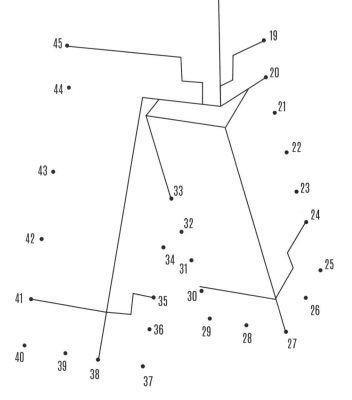

4.

What do you see?

_____

Having trouble guessing character!? Clue: when killed he drop 0-2 pieces of rotting flesh. Disgusting!

MAZE RUNNER

START

Can you find a way through the maze? Be careful not to fall into the lava!

GAME OVER

GAME OVER

FINISH

HOW TO DRAW A CREEPER

Grab yourself a pen and draw each step to create the ultimate Creeper drawing.

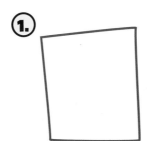

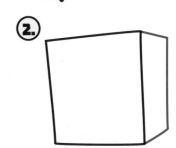

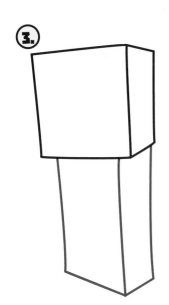

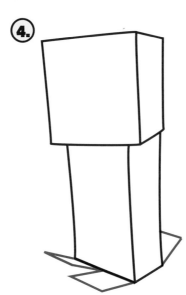

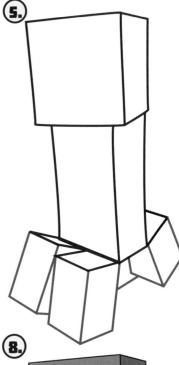

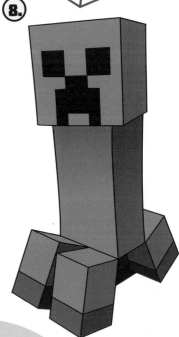

Charged creepers are created when lightning strikes within 3-4 blocks of a normal creeper.

DRAWN BY:..

WORDSEARCH

 6. Can you find these Minecraft-related words? You'll need your hunting skills to find some of them!

S	K	E	L	E	T	O	N	A	D
R	C	O	W	P	O	T	H	S	I
M	E	V	F	Z	P	L	A	Y	A
P	G	S	W	M	F	X	G	Z	M
V	C	U	P	U	E	S	X	X	O
T	H	I	N	A	C	R	A	E	N
O	E	G	P	W	W	R	U	V	D
N	S	L	Y	O	D	N	E	E	N
G	T	R	Z	G	H	O	S	T	B
W	I	T	H	E	R	T	O	S	E

AXE	DIAMOND	SKELETON
COW	GHOST	STEVE
CHEST	RESPAWN	WITHER

7. Can you see five Creepers lurking in the image below?

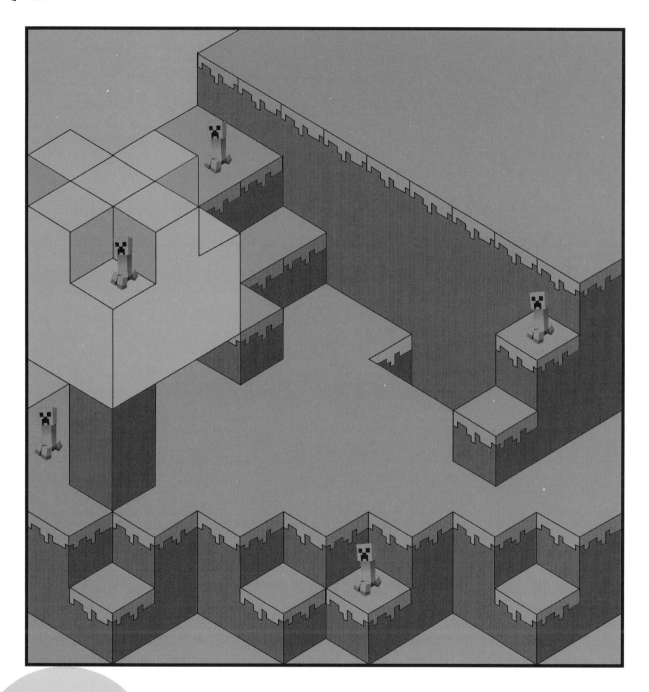

A creeper will explode if they fall on a player from a certain height.

DOT-TO-DOT

8. Draw a line from dot to dot to complete the picture.

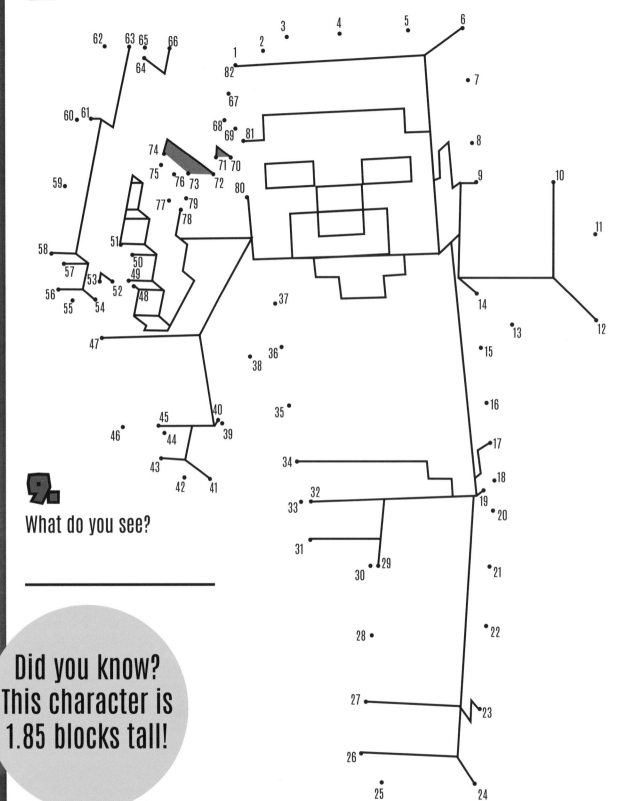

9.

What do you see?

_____

Did you know?
This character is
1.85 blocks tall!

DOUBLE TROUBLE

10. Copy the drawings across into the blank spaces to see two complete pictures of Steve ready for battle.

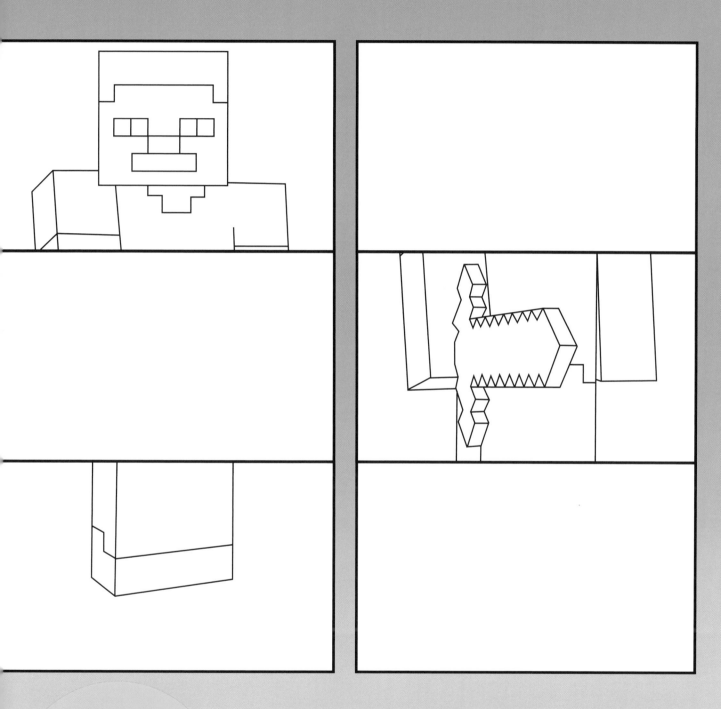

Have you noticed something about Steve's shirt? It's untucked on the left-hand side!

CROSSWORD

11. Can you solve our special crossword? Good luck!

ACROSS

5. To write a book in the game, you need a book and...
6. The man who came up with Minecraft!
7. Found in abandoned mineshafts and slows you down!
9. A block that will burn forever when you set fire to it.
10. You use this as electricity.
12. You do this to make the most of the blocks and materials in the game.
13. You need a furnace for this.
15. You need one of these to travel on rails!
16. Craft one of these and you'll be able to sleep!

17. You can use this to repair tools, weapons and armour.

DOWN

1. These are the people you can trade with.
2. A mob that explodes when it gets too close!
3. A cow that you'll only find in the mushroom biome.
4. A boss mob that you'll only find at the End.
8. Jungle, desert and ice plains are all types of this.
11. One of the game modes.
14. A boss mob with three heads.
15. The name of the company that publishes Minecraft.

12. RIDDLE-ME-THIS

I look like a tree
But I'm not covered in leaves.
I have an explosive personality and I like to hiss,
Once I find you, I rarely miss.
What am I?

ANSWER _____

BUILD PLANNER

There's nothing better than seeing your designs come to life, and we love using this build planner in helping to produce our creations!

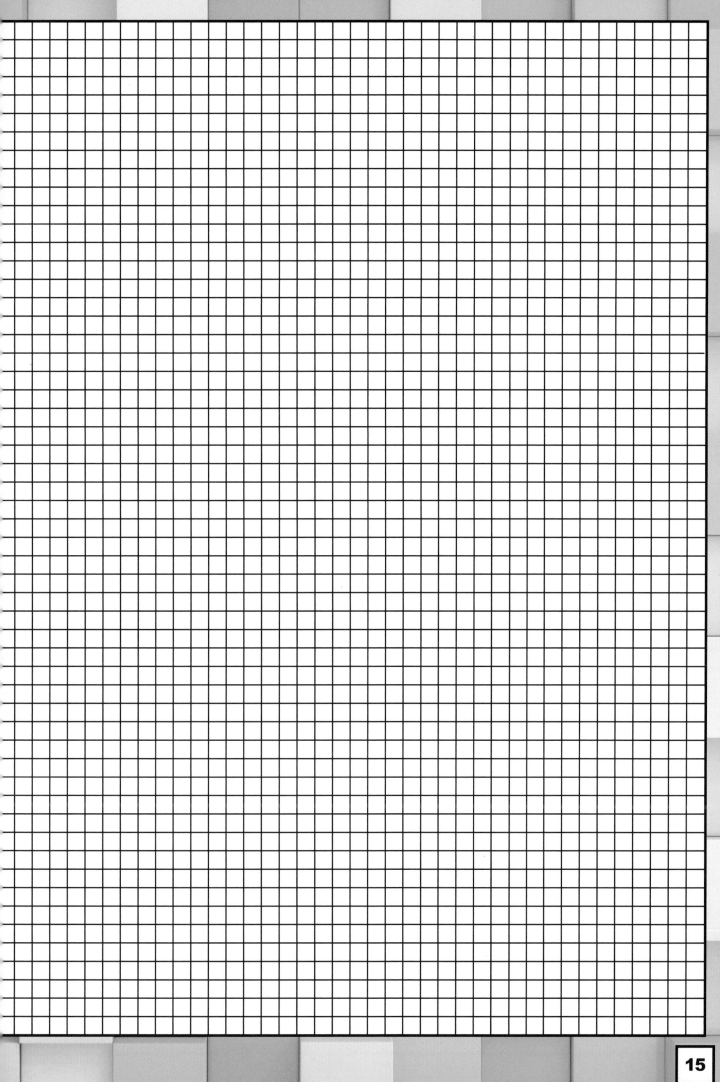

RIDDLE-ME-THIS

13. Steve needs exactly 4 litres of water to make potions. He has a 3 and a 5 litre potion bottle, each bottle has no markings except for that which gives you its total volume. You also have a running tap. He must use the bottles and the tap in such a way as to exactly measure out 4 litres of water. How is this done?

3 litre   4 litre   5 litre

ANSWER _____

_____

_____

_____

_____

COLOUR ME IN

Can you draw a sword on the grid? Each square on the sword represents one square in the grid. We have started an outline for you.

COLOUR-BY-NUMBER

Legend:
1 5 9
2 6 10
3 7
4 8

MAZE RUNNER

14. Enter through door 1. Exit the maze through door 2. Closed doors are locked. Good luck!

DRAGON HUNTER

15. Follow the correct path to hit the Dragon. Be careful not to miss as only one arrow will hit the target.

MAZE RUNNER

MAZE RUNNER

16. Find your way out of this desolate desert maze!

START

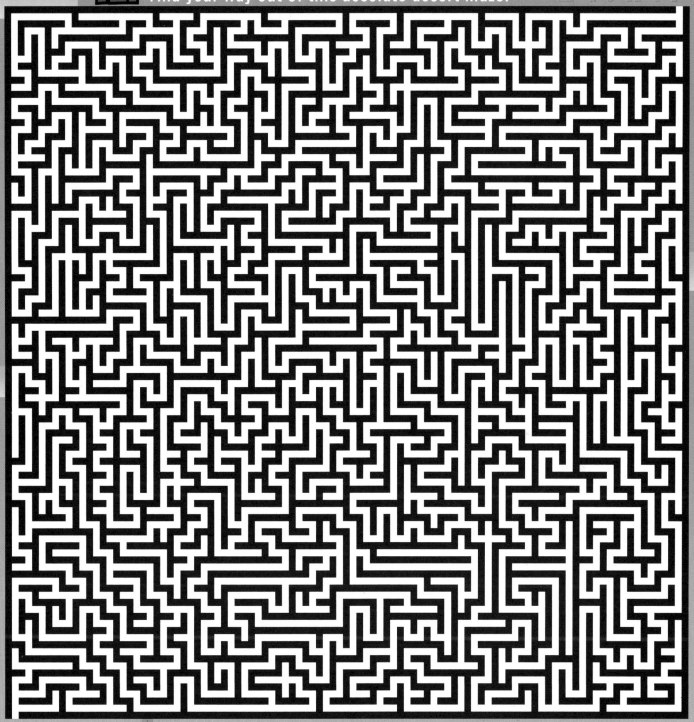

FINISH

CREEPER FACE CHALLENGE

17.

Can you draw the creeper face shape in one go?

Rule 1. You are not allowed to lift the pen off the page.
Rule 2. You are not allowed to go over the same line.

MAZE RUNNER

18. Using stairs and ladders try to find the way from point 1 to point 2. Do not jump or climb up!

FACE BUILDER

Let's see how many faces of Minecraft characters you can draw in the boxes below? Colour each square in each box to create your favourite characters.

ANAGRAMS

19. Can you unscramble the letters to see what words we meant to write?!

1	FANMETRIC	_ _ _ _ _ _ _ _ _
2	REDEN DOGRAN	_ _ _ _ _ _ _ _ _ _ _
3	THENCRAKER	_ _ _ _ _ _ _ _ _ _
4	DROVERLOW	_ _ _ _ _ _ _ _ _
5	RESTEDNO	_ _ _ _ _ _ _ _
6	BIZMOE	_ _ _ _ _ _
7	WRITHE	_ _ _ _ _ _
8	FORKWIRES	_ _ _ _ _ _ _ _ _

RIDDLE-ME-THIS

20. Can you match the riddle to the Minecraft object?

1. WHAT HAS TO BE BROKEN BEFORE YOU CAN USE IT?

2. WHAT DO YOU GET WHEN YOU DIVIDE THE CIRCUMFERENCE OF YOUR JACK 'O' LANTERN BY ITS DIAMETER?

3. WHAT'S FULL OF HOLES BUT STILL HOLDS WATER?

4. WHAT CAN RUN BUT CAN'T WALK?

SPONGE

WATER

EGG

PUMKIN PIE

21. Draw a line from dot to dot to complete the picture!

22.

What do you see?

_____

These characters are unique in that they can pick up and move certain types of blocks!

1 2 3

72

71 70   5 4
68 69   6 7

66 67   8 9

65 48   23 10

49   24 22

64 47
50

25
35 34 27 21
46 45   26 11

63
51 44 36 33

37

62 43 20
52 38 28
32 12

42 39
53
61 40 29 19
54 31
41 30
13
55 18
60 56 17
57 16
59 58 15 14

MAZE RUNNER

23. Can you find a way through the Creeper face maze?

MINECRAFT JOKES!

DID YOU HEAR ABOUT THE MINECRAFT MOVIE?

It was a blockbuster!

WHY DOESN'T MINECRAFT COME WITH A MANUAL?

Because the developers had writer's block!

WHY ARE THERE NO CARS IN MINECRAFT?

Because the roads are always blocked off!

WHERE DO GHASTS LIVE?

The Nether-lands!

HOW DO STEVE AND ALEX GET THEIR EXERCISE?

They go for a run around the block!

DID YOU HEAR ABOUT THE CREEPER'S BIRTHDAY PARTY?

It was a blast!

ANSWERS

1.

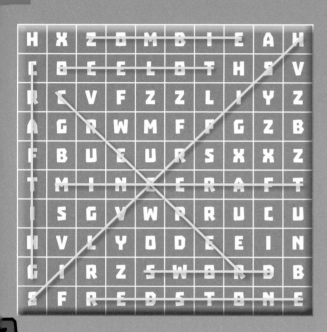

2.

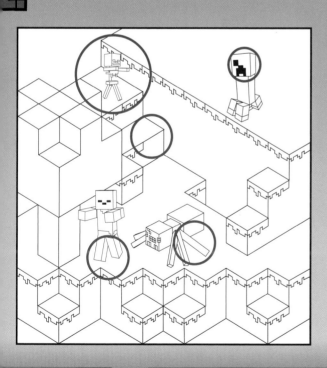

3.

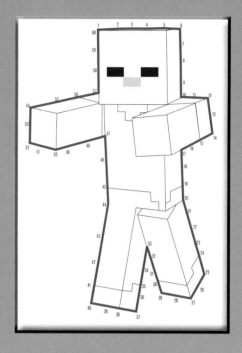

4. Zombie

5.

6.

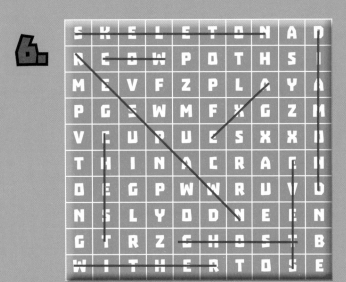

S	K	E	L	E	T	O	N	A	D
R	C	O	W	P	O	T	H	S	I
M	E	V	F	Z	P	L	A	Y	A
P	G	S	W	M	F	X	G	Z	M
V	C	U	D	U	E	S	X	X	O
T	H	I	N	A	C	R	A	G	H
O	E	G	P	W	W	R	U	V	D
N	S	L	Y	D	D	N	E	E	N
G	T	R	Z	G	H	O	S	T	B
W	I	T	H	E	R	T	O	S	E

7.

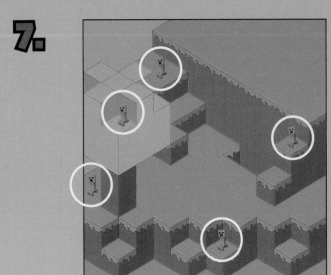

8.

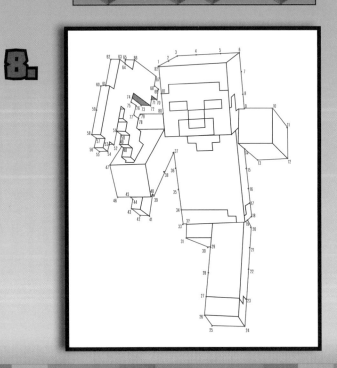

9. Steve

10.

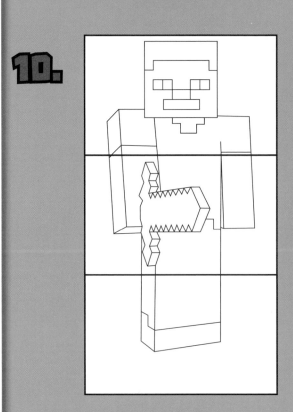

11.

A Creeper

1. Fill the 5 litre bottle from the tap
2. Empty the 5 litre bottle into the 3 litre bottle > leaving 2 litres in the 5 litre bottle.
3. Pour away the contents of the 3 litre bottle.
4. Fill the 3 litre bottle with the 2 litres from the 5 litre bottle > leaving 2 litres in the 3 litre bottle.
5. Fill the 5 litre bottle from the tap.
6. Fill the remaining 1 litre space in the 3 litre can from the 5 litre bottle.

Leaving 4 litres in the 5 litre bottle.

14.

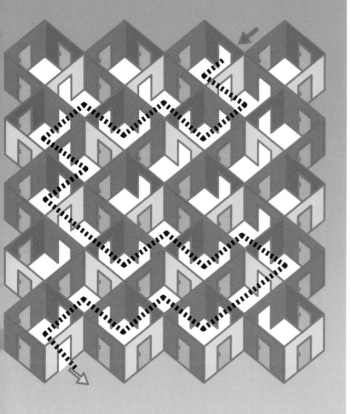

15.

16.

17.

18.

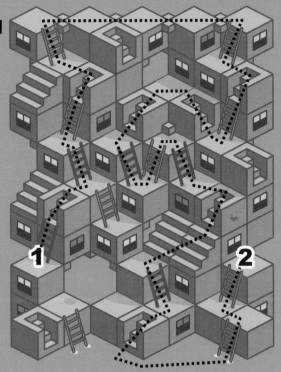

19.

1	MINECRAFT	6	ZOMBIE
2	ENDER DRAGON	7	WITHER
3	NETHERRACK	8	FIREWORKS
4	OVERWORLD		
5	REDSTONE		

20.

1. EGG

2. Pumkin Pie

3. Sponge

4. Water

21.

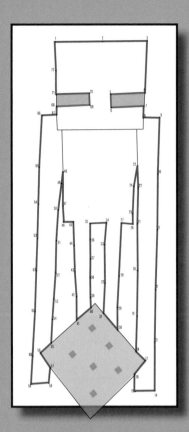

22. Enderman

23.